The Galapagos Islands

Diana Noonan

The Galapagos Islands

Text: Diana Noonan
Publishers: Tania Mazzeo and Eliza Webb
Series consultant: Amanda Sutera
Hands on Heads Consulting
Editors: Jarrah Moore and Sarah Layton
Project editor: Annabel Smith
Designer: Leigh Ashforth
Project designer: Danielle Maccarone
Maps: Wayne Murphy
Diagram: Fabian Slongo
Permissions researcher: Lumina Datamatics
Production controller: Renee Tome

Acknowledgements
We would like to thank the following for permission to reproduce copyright material:

Front cover, p. 2: FOTOGRIN/Shutterstock.com; p. 4: iStock.com/E+/4FR; p. 5: Andrew Peacock/Stone/Getty Images; p. 6: Getty Images/Getty Images News/Getty Images; p. 9 (top): Juan Carlos Munoz/Nature Picture Library, (bottom): Elena Mirolyubova | DreamsTime.com; p. 32, p. 10 (top): Tui De Roy, p. 10 (bottom): FLICKETTI/Shutterstock.com; p. 11 (top): Thomas ROUSSEL/Alamy Stock Photo, (bottom), Content page p.3: nwdph/Shutterstock.com; p. 12: NadyaRa/Shutterstock.com; p. 13 (top left): Tui De Roy, (top right): Angela/Adobe Stock Photos, (first middle right): Longjourneys/Adobe Stock Photos, (second middle right): Angela Perryman/Dreamstime.com, (third middle right), title page p.1: Femke van den Bos/Shutterstock.com, (fourth middle right): iStock.com/Gerald Corsi, (bottom right), Back cover p.1: Betty Sederquist/Adobe Stock Photos, (bottom left): KrystynaSzulecka/Alamy Stock Photo; p. 14: Gary Calton/Alamy Stock Photo; p. 15 (top): CPA Media Pte Ltd/Alamy Stock Photo, (bottom): iStock.com/E+/guenterguni; p. 16 (top): mauritius images GmbH/Alamy Stock Photo, (bottom) robertharding/Alamy Stock Photo; p. 17 (top): Tui De Roy/Nature Picture Library, (bottom): pb_pictures/Adobe Stock Photos; p. 18: Jeff Vanuga/Nature Picture Library; p. 19 (top): Gilbert S. Grant/Shutterstock.com, (bottom): npavlov/Shutterstock.com; p. 20 (top): Minden Pictures/Alamy Stock Photo, (bottom) Nature Picture Library/Alamy Stock Photo; p. 21: Pete Oxford/Nature Picture Library; p. 22: Cavan Images/Alamy Stock Photo; p. 23 (top): Tui De Roy/Minden pictures, (bottom left): ©Stubblefield Photography/Shutterstock.com, (bottom right): Agami Photo Agency/Shutterstock.com; p. 24 (top): Cavan Images/Alamy Stock Photo, (bottom): iStock.com/zysman; p. 25: photo doesn't match with spreadsheet description; p. 26 (top): Don Mammoser/Shutterstock.com, (bottom): Robert Fried/Alamy Stock Photo; p. 27: Ecuadorpostales/Shutterstock.com; p. 28 (top): Daniel Llao Calvet/Getty Images, (bottom): Interfoto/Sartorius/akg-images; p. 29: SL-Photography/Shutterstock.com; p. 30: Jess Kraft/Shutterstock.com.

Every effort has been made to trace and acknowledge copyright. However, if any infringement has occurred, the publishers tender their apologies and invite the copyright holders to contact them.

NovaStar

ISBN 978 0 17 033478 5

Cengage Learning Australia
Level 5, 80 Dorcas Street
Southbank VIC 3006 Australia
Phone: 1300 790 853
Email: aust.nelsonprimary@cengage.com

For learning solutions, visit **cengage.com.au**

Printed in China by 1010 Printing International Ltd
1 2 3 4 5 6 7 29 28 27 26 25

Nelson acknowledges the Traditional Owners and Custodians of the lands of all First Nations Peoples. We pay respect to Elders past and present, and extend that respect to all First Nations Peoples today.

Contents

A Unique Environment

The Galapagos Islands are a group of islands, or archipelago (pronounced *ar-kuh-pel-uh-go*), in the Pacific Ocean, almost 1000 kilometres from the shore of Ecuador, South America. The archipelago consists of 19 large islands and over 100 islets (very small islands) and rocks. Although the Galapagos Islands are a part of Ecuador, it takes people three days by ship, or a little over two hours by plane, to travel to the islands from the rest of Ecuador. This makes the Galapagos Islands very **remote**.

The Galapagos Islands are part of Ecuador.

The Galapagos Islands are surrounded by the blue waters of the Pacific Ocean.

The **climate** of the Galapagos Islands is unique. Most land near the equator is always warm. But the seawater around the Galapagos Islands can be cold, and air blowing off the cold seawater cools the nearby islands.

The Galapagos Islands' unique climate is one of the reasons it contains such special **ecosystems**. The many unusual plants and animals that make up these ecosystems can't be found anywhere else in the world. **Reserves** help to protect them.

Marine iguanas enjoy the sunshine and warm rocks in the Galapagos Islands.

How the Galapagos Islands Formed

The islands of the Galapagos archipelago began as undersea volcanoes millions of years ago. The volcanoes erupted from a "hotspot" – a weak place in Earth's **crust** where lava bursts through. This is known as the "Galapagos hotspot".

As lava flowed down the sides of the volcanoes, it cooled. Over time, the cold lava was worn down by the weather into areas of soil where plants could grow.

An undersea volcano sends clouds of hot ash above the water's surface as it erupts.

The Galapagos Islands lie along a tectonic plate called the Nazca Plate. Tectonic plates are massive slabs of rock, kilometres thick, that are part of Earth's crust.

Tectonic plates rest on Earth's **mantle**, and they move very slowly over time. As the Nazca Plate moves, it keeps carrying islands away from the hotspot where they were created. The oldest islands are furthest from the Galapagos hotspot. The newest islands are closest to it. Over millions of years, new islands will continue to be created over the Galapagos hotspot.

On the move

Most of the time, tectonic plates move too slowly for us to notice. But we sometimes feel their movement as an earthquake.

The Creation of New Galapagos Islands

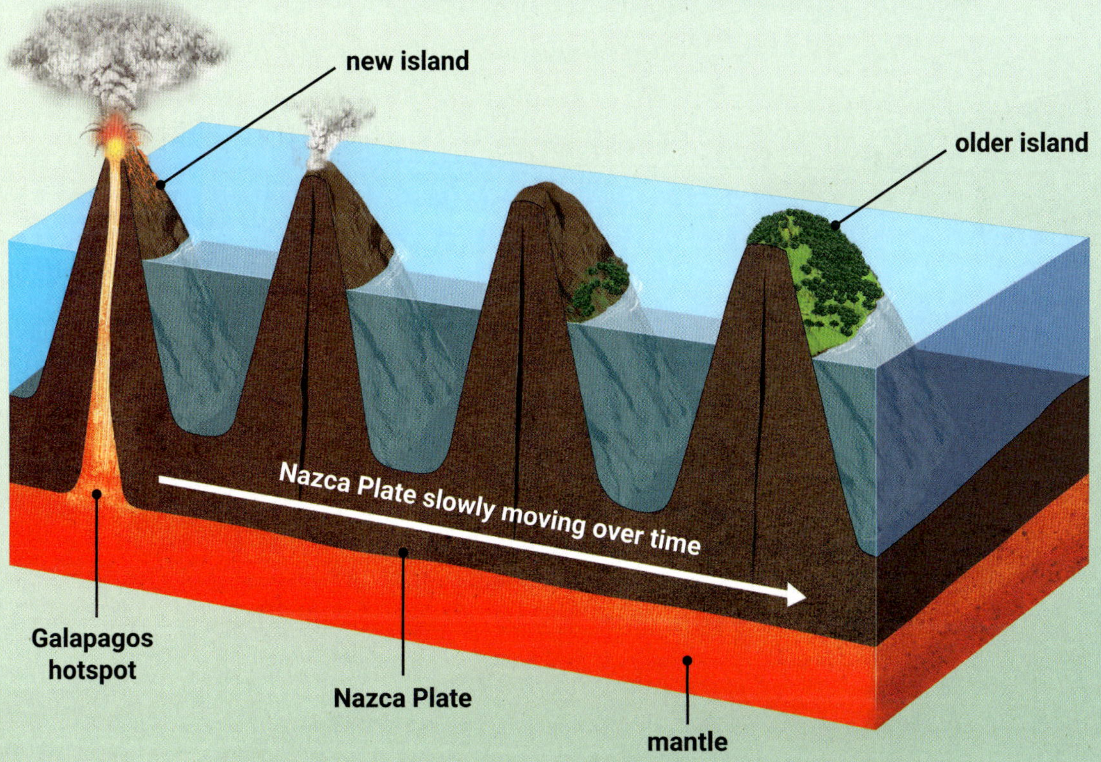

New islands are created over the Galapagos hotspot, then slowly carried away by the movement of the Nazca Plate.

Islands of the Galapagos

The Galapagos Islands make up over 8000 square kilometres of land. Ninety-seven per cent of this land is a reserve called the Galapagos National Park. The reserve helps protect the islands' plants and animals. The sea around the Galapagos Islands is also protected. A **marine reserve**, almost half the size of Ecuador, helps keep the Galapagos's marine animals and plants safe.

Three Per Cent

Just 3 per cent of the Galapagos Islands is not part of the reserve. People live and work in the non-reserve areas.

The sea around the Galapagos Islands is protected by a marine reserve.

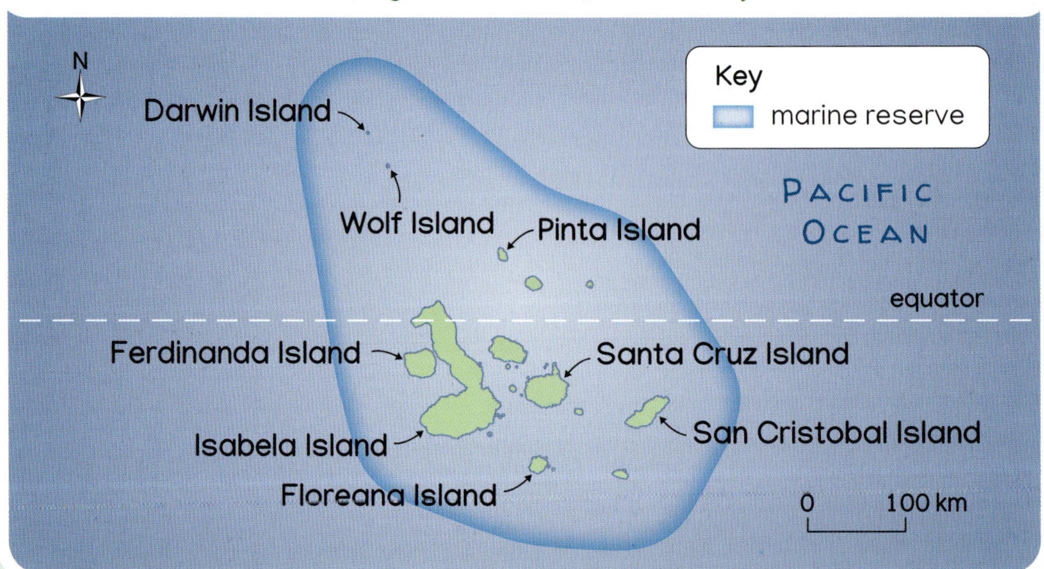

Each of the Galapagos islands has its own special character. Older islands have more vegetation than younger islands because some of their volcanic rock has worn down into soil. Younger islands are more bare and volcanic. Some volcanoes on younger islands are still erupting.

Let's have a closer look at some of the islands of the Galapagos together.

Isabela Island

Isabela is the largest and highest of the Galapagos Islands. It was formed by lava erupting out of its six volcanoes. Five of these volcanoes are still active. One of Isabela's volcanoes, Sierra Negra, has the second largest **crater** in the world.

Hikers gaze at the Sierra Negra volcano crater.

San Cristobal Island

San Cristobal is one of four Galapagos Islands where people may live and farm. It is also the oldest of the Galapagos Islands. It was formed by four volcanoes that are now extinct. The island has lush green **highlands**, bush, farms and a freshwater lake. It is famous for the sea lions that laze about the streets of its largest town, Puerto Baquerizo Moreno.

A sea lion dozes on a bench in Puerto Baquerizo Moreno.

Fernandina Island

Fernandina is the youngest of the Galapagos Islands. It is less than a million years old. It sits right in the middle of the Galapagos hotspot, and was formed when La Cumbre Volcano erupted out of the sea. No one lives on the almost **barren** island, and its volcano is still active.

Fernandina Island's volcano erupts.

Darwin Island

Darwin Island is 21 kilometres away from its closest neighbour, Wolf Island. This makes it the most remote of the Galapagos Islands. Darwin Island is the tip of a massive volcano that erupted over 1.6 million years ago. The water around Darwin Island is home to sea turtles, dolphins, manta rays and large schools of hammerhead sharks.

Hammerhead sharks swim off the coast of Darwin Island.

Santa Cruz Island

More people live on Santa Cruz than on any of the other Galapagos Islands. It is home to around 17 000 people, and has a **port**, a hospital and a scientific research centre. The volcano that formed Santa Cruz Island is now dormant.

Many people live on Santa Cruz Island.

Pinta Island

For many years, **native** plants and animals on Pinta Island were destroyed by non-native animals, particularly goats. These non-native animals ate the plants that the native animals depended on for food and shelter. Now, the non-native animals have been removed from the island, and the wildlife of Pinta Island is recovering.

Galapagos hawks can be found on Pinta Island.

Climate and Habitat Zones

Land that is close to the equator is usually warm all year. This is because the sea around the equator is warm. The Galapagos Islands are an exception. Both warm and cold ocean currents flow past the islands, depending on the time of year.

From December to May, air blowing off warm seawater creates a hot wet season. At this time of year, temperatures are around 27 to 32 degrees Celsius. From June to November, air blowing off cold seawater creates a cooler and windier dry season. At this time of year, temperatures are around 21 to 27 degrees Celsius. The Galapagos Islands' wettest month is March, when about 5 cm of rain falls.

Ocean Currents

Ocean water is always on the move. It travels in wide currents that are like rivers within the sea. These currents can be cold or warm. Ocean currents help cool or heat the air and the land around them.

Rain clouds gather above Santa Cruz Island.

The Galapagos Islands' climate and landscape creates five different "habitat zones". These are areas that each have their own special features, plants and animal life.

Habitat Zone	Features	Common Plants and Animals
Marine	• reefs • deep ocean • undersea volcanoes	sharks, rays, tropical fish
Shore	• rocky shores • salty lagoons • sandy beaches • mangroves and other salt-loving plants	Pacific green sea turtle
Arid	• dry ground • rain only in the warm wet season	blue-footed booby
Transition	• small shrubs and trees • low-growing herbs	wild Galapagos tomatoes
Humid	• **cloud forest**	orchids, moss, epiphytes (plants that grow on other plants)

Animals of the Galapagos

The Galapagos Islands are home to some of the most unusual and rare animals in the world. It is believed that some of their ancestors (such as rats and mice) may have floated to the islands millions of years ago on **driftwood** or on natural rafts of floating plants. The ancestors of animals that are good swimmers, such as sea turtles and penguins, may have managed to swim to the islands, carried along on strong ocean currents.

There are few predators on the Galapagos Islands, so the animals there are not often in danger. Even today, animals on the Galapagos Islands are unlikely to move away from people watching them.

Tourists take photos of a giant tortoise on Santa Cruz Island.

Charles Darwin

Charles Darwin was a famous scientist who spent many years studying the plants and animals of the Galapagos Islands. He was the first person to realise that plants and animals change when the environment and food supplies change.

The sea animals of the Galapagos Islands, such as penguins, sea lions and seals, thrive in the cold ocean currents. Reptiles, such as iguanas, tortoises and sea turtles, use the heat of the sun to warm up their bodies.

Over millions of years, the climate of the Galapagos Islands has changed. The animals have slowly **evolved** to suit the new conditions.

A land iguana enjoys the sunshine in the Galapagos Islands.

Marine Iguana

The Galapagos Islands' marine iguana is the only lizard in the world that spends most of its time in or beside the sea. It swims, and it holds onto underwater rocks with its claws while it grazes on **algae**.

A marine iguana swims underwater.

Galapagos Penguin

The Galapagos penguin is one of the smallest penguins in the world, and the only penguin to make its nest close to the equator. It feeds off fish that live in the cold-water currents around the islands.

Galapagos penguins swim together.

Galapagos Tortoise

The Galapagos tortoise is the largest tortoise in the world. These giant tortoises can weigh up to 400 kilograms, and they live in the wild for more than 100 years. There are 15 different species of Galapagos tortoises native to different islands. Some have a dip in the neck of their shells that allows them to stretch up high to feed on cactuses.

A Galapagos tortoise munches on a cactus.

Blue-Footed Booby

The blue-footed booby is a sea bird that dives and swims underwater to catch fish. Each year, half of all the blue-footed booby nests in the world are made on the Galapagos Islands.

A blue-footed booby chick stays near its parents.

Plants of the Galapagos

The Galapagos Islands are home to a diverse range of plants, many of which are not found anywhere else in the world! Some first reached the Galapagos Islands by floating on the wind or the ocean. Some arrived as seeds that had been swallowed by birds and "planted" along with the birds' droppings. Over millions of years, the plants have evolved to suit the islands' unique ecosystems.

A bird soars over the mangroves of Santa Cruz Island.

Mangroves

Mangroves are common in the Galapagos Islands, as well as in other parts of the world. Most plants grow in fresh water, but mangroves grow in salt water close to the shore and in **estuaries**.

The mangrove plant's unique roots and leaves allow it to grow in salt water.

Lava Cactus

The lava cactus is only found in the Galapagos Islands. It is one of the first plants that starts growing on young volcanic islands. Its roots grow down into cracks in the hardened lava in search of moisture.

The lava cactus can grow in hardened lava.

Giant Daisy Tree

When the Galapagos Islands daisy tree first arrived from the continent of South America, it was just a small plant. Over millions of years, with no animals to eat it, it evolved to grow taller. Now it grows as tall as a tree.

Giant daisy trees don't look much like daisies any more.

Red and Green Algae

Cold water filled with plant food helps the Galapagos Islands algae to grow. Some algae is red and some is green. Marine iguanas, which feed on the algae, have different coloured skin depending on which algae they eat.

A marine iguana snacks on green algae.

People of the Galapagos

Scientists

Each year, scientists from all over the world come to the Galapagos Islands to study the natural environment. The islands' volcanoes, special ocean currents and unique plants and animals are like a living laboratory. Scientists hope that, by putting their skills together, they will uncover the islands' natural secrets.

Scientists examine a Galapagos hawk in the wild.

The most well-known scientific centre on the Galapagos Islands is the Charles Darwin Research Station. The station is on the island of Santa Cruz, and is an important centre for the study of **conservation** and **sustainability**.

Volcanologists

Volcanologists study volcanoes – how a volcano behaved in the past and if and how it may erupt in the future. The Galapagos Islands are of special interest to volcanologists because both dormant and active volcanoes are found within a reasonably small area.

In 2020, volcanologists studying Galapagos Islands volcanoes made an important discovery – one that could help keep people safe in the future. They found that volcanoes that have always erupted in the same, safe way, year after year, can change. These volcanoes may one day become highly explosive and very dangerous to humans. Because of the Galapagos Islands volcanologists, people living near volcanoes can now receive more accurate warnings about eruptions.

Researchers who spend a lot of time on the islands also need accurate information about volcanic activity.

Biologists

Biologists study humans, plants, animals and the different environments they live in. The Galapagos Islands are important to biologists because the remote location means fewer people live there than in many other parts of the world. And the fewer people there are, the less they use the islands' **resources** and change the natural environment. For this reason, some biologists say the Galapagos Islands are like "a glimpse into the past".

A biologist measures a Galapagos tortoise.

The Galapagos Islands' remote location also means that when different plants and animals reached it, they had to evolve more quickly to survive in their new environment, compared to plants and animals in other parts of the world. This was because there was nowhere else for them to find food and shelter.

Finches Adapting

During a major drought on the Galapagos Islands in 1977, biologists were able to show that some animals are better than others at **adapting** to changes. They noticed that ground finches with bigger beaks could crack open the hard seeds of the plants that still grew in the very dry conditions. Smaller-beaked finches couldn't do this, and began to starve.

The large ground finch (left) has a bigger beak than the small ground finch (right).

Botanists

Botanists are scientists who study plants. The Galapagos Islands have many plants that are found nowhere else in the world. The islands are also interesting to botanists because they have several different "plant zones" within a small distance. Plant zones are areas with their own climate and soil types.

Botanists measure an opuntia cactus.

Bird Gardeners

Charles Darwin also made an important discovery about plants after visiting the Galapagos Islands. He learnt that many seeds could still sprout after they had been eaten by birds. When these seeds came out in a bird's droppings, they were ready to grow.

A frigatebird soars over the Galapagos Islands.

Residents

The first people to live on the Galapagos Islands from the 1500s to the 1800s were pirates, shipwrecked sailors and men who came to hunt whales. Later, the government of Ecuador sent prisoners to live and work on the islands. Today, the Galapagos Islands' population is around 28 000 people and steadily growing. Most of the people who live there speak Spanish.

People who live on the Galapagos Islands fish and grow food on the islands. This is necessary because food brought by boat from the rest of South America has to travel a long way, and is very expensive.

The only islands that people live on in the Galapagos Islands are Santa Cruz, San Cristobal, Isabela and Floreana. The homes on these islands are in special zones set aside for towns and villages, which take up only 3 per cent of the islands' land.

Almost half of the islands' residents work in tourism. Others depend on farming and fishing.

Fishermen from Isabela Island work on their boat outside the Galapagos marine reserve.

Tourists

Each year, thousands of tourists from all over the world visit the Galapagos Islands. Santa Cruz is the island most tourists visit first.

Tourists get to know the islands' unusual land and sea life by hiking, snorkelling, kayaking and sailing. Some tourists volunteer to help with conservation projects.

Puerto Ayora is the biggest town on Santa Cruz Island.

Land and marine reserves help keep the islands' plants and wildlife safe, but tourism also causes some serious problems.

A tour group looks over a dried lava field on the Galapagos Islands.

Protection Laws

Laws exist to help protect the natural environments of the Galapagos Islands from people. The number of visitors to the Galapagos Islands each year is limited. Tourists go with a trained guide when they go exploring.

A World-Famous Habitat

The natural habitats of the Galapagos Islands are some of the most important habitats in the world. The islands are a place where scientists and others come to learn more about nature and how animals and plants adapt to survive changing conditions. The islands are also a place that thousands of tourists enjoy visiting, and a home to the community of people who live there.

People must continue to learn to live and work together with nature to protect this unique place.

Should There Be Tourists on the Galapagos Islands?

by **Sean**

Hi, everyone. Thanks for checking in on our school's weekly blog – and for taking an interest in whether tourists should be visiting the Galapagos Islands!

The Galapagos Islands are a remote and very special archipelago in the Pacific Ocean. They are full of amazing and rare animal and plant life that is of incredible importance to science. That's why I believe the islands are not a place that tourists should be visiting.

The first tourists arrived in 1934 – and there were just 200 of them. Thirty-one years later, in 1965, 4500 tourists visited. In 2022, over 200 000 sightseers came to explore the islands. Tourists bring benefits to the islands, but also problems. And I think the problems are too big to ignore.

This photo shows tourists arriving on the Galapagos Islands by boat in 1970.

Most Galapagos Islands tourists like to take boat tours to get from island to island and see as many different and amazing animals as possible. But boat engine noise disturbs both marine and land animals. Also, when paint flakes off the sides of boats, marine animals can end up eating the flakes and the harmful chemicals they contain. Engine oil from boats can also pollute marine environments.

Tourists need places to stay, and more and more hotels are being built in the Galapagos Islands. Those hotels produce wastewater and rubbish. There is a danger that some of it will end up in the sea, or in the islands' other natural habitats. If it does, it can harm plants and animals.

Galapagos tourists often take part in activities such as horse riding, camping, snorkelling and kayaking. But at the moment, no one really knows if these activities are good for the islands' environment. By the time scientists have the answers, it may be too late to reverse any damage.

I believe tourists should not be allowed to visit the Galapagos Islands. The environment in this special part of the world should be only for the plants, animals, scientists and people who already live there. The rest of us can enjoy the Galapagos Islands by looking at photos.

I look forward to your comments!
Sean

Glossary

adapting (*verb*)	becoming used to something, such as weather patterns
algae (*noun*)	simple plants like seaweed that grow in or near water
barren (*adjective*)	bare, with no plants able to grow in the soil
climate (*noun*)	the weather patterns throughout the year
cloud forest (*noun*)	a forest in a high area where clouds often pass through the treetops
conservation (*noun*)	the protection of wildlife and the environment
crater (*noun*)	a large bowl-shaped hole in the top of a volcano
crust (*noun*)	the outer layer of rock around Earth
driftwood (*noun*)	wood that ends up on land after floating, or drifting, in the water
ecosystems (*noun*)	communities of plants and animals living together in an environment
estuaries (*noun*)	the parts of large rivers that open up to the sea
evolved (*verb*)	changed over a long period of time
highlands (*noun*)	areas with hills or mountains
mantle (*noun*)	the layer of Earth below the tectonic plates of Earth's rocky crust
marine reserve (*noun*)	an area of the ocean where the plants and wildlife are protected
native (*adjective*)	belonging to an area
port (*noun*)	a city or town where ships can stop
remote (*adjective*)	far away from other people and towns
reserves (*noun*)	areas where the plants and wildlife are protected
resources (*noun*)	supplies of things that are useful, such as water
sustainability (*noun*)	ways of using materials that make sure they are still available in the future

Index